Everything You Need to Know About

MEDIA VIOLENCE

Children's television programs have about twenty to twenty-five violent acts every hour.

· THE NEED TO KNOW LIBRARY ·

Everything You Need to Know About

MEDIA VIOLENCE

Kathleen J. Edgar

THE ROSEN PUBLISHING GROUP, INC.
NEW YORK

To my late father, Donald, for giving me the footsteps in which to follow. And to my mother, Nancy, and sister, Susan, who continue to inspire me.

Published in 1998 by The Rosen Publishing Group, Inc.
29 East 21st Street, New York, NY 10010

First Edition
Copyright © 1998 by The Rosen Publishing Group, Inc.

Library of Congress Cataloging-in-Publication Data

Edgar, Kathy.
  Everything you need to know about media violence / Kathy Edgar.
     p.   cm.-- (The need to know library)
  Includes bibliographical references (p.) and index.
  ISBN 0-8239-2568-4
  1. Violence in mass media--Juvenile literature.   I. Title.
  II. Series.
  P96.V5E34 1998
  303.6--dc21   97-32823
                                        CIP
                                        AC

Manufactured in the United States of America.

Contents

Introduction

The Media Violence Debate

Violence. It is found in our homes; it threatens our streets and communities; its presence in schools makes it difficult for students to get an education. It is found in books; it is heard in music on the radio; it fills the screens of televisions and movie theaters. It is featured in video games and on the Internet. Today's society is the most violent in U.S. history. People hurt or kill each other over drugs, gym shoes, for showing disrespect, or just to know what it feels like. Violent crime by teenagers is a major problem.

People want the violence to stop. They want to understand why it happens. While violence occurs for many reasons, some people believe that violence in the media is a major influence. The media—which includes television, movies, music, radio, newspapers, magazines, and the Internet—provides information to people throughout the world. People are concerned that the media spend too much time focusing on horrible acts of violence and not enough time on positive events. People want the media to use better judgment in how they portray violence.

Among the biggest complaints about media violence is that it is gratuitous—or excessive and unecessary—and that its full effects or consequences are not shown. Gratuitous violence can include graphic or gory stabbings, shootings, beheadings, rapes, or other grisly acts that are shown or described in full detail, but are not essential to the story. Gratuitous violence is used to shock people. Gratuitous violence is often depicted without the violent person facing the consequences of the action. The media, on the other hand, say the violence they depict is based on real life. Some media producers believe that people are interested in violence because they buy products or tune into programs that feature it.

In movies and television shows with gratuitous violence, the full effects of the violence (other than the bloodshed) are rarely shown either. We never see how the victim and the perpetrator cope after the violent act or what effect the violence has on their families, friends, and communities. Violent content is so high in some products (particularly music, television programs, and films) that warning labels are used.

Studies show that media violence is harmful to teenagers for several reasons. When you see so much violence in the media, you may begin to think that it is more common in real life than it really is. When you see so much of it throughout all media, you may grow accustomed to it and accept it as a normal part of life. You may stop feeling upset about violence in your own life, family, and community. Or you may begin to feel as indifferent toward real violence as you do about fictional violence. This is called desensitizing. It can also lead to feelings of cynicism—believing that everyone is motivated by their own self-interest.

Studies also indicate that media violence can cause people to feel contempt or disgust for others. It also encourages negative stereotypes about certain groups of people. Stereotypes are characteristics that some people attribute to others based on heritage, gender, religion, sexual orientation, where they live, or how much money they have. Many stereotypes are negative traits and don't accurately describe the people in that group.

Minorities are often stereotyped on television as violent criminals. Stereotypes are often based on prejudice—judging someone you don't even know because you think they will act or be a certain way. Stereotypes occur because people lack knowledge about other groups. When stereotypes are shown again and again in the media, some people believe them and don't learn the truth for themselves.

Some people want the government to reduce the amount of violence depicted in the media. Some want the media themselves to clean up their products. Others believe that no one should try to influence, censor, or edit what the media present. They think people should decide for themselves what they listen to, watch, or read. They argue that if a person doesn't like the content of an article or program, for example, he or she can refuse to read it or can simply turn it off. The First Amendment to the U.S. Constitution guarantees freedom of speech. Many people want to be able to decide for themselves what is offensive.

However, parents are often less concerned about censorship when it comes to what their children watch, hear, or read. Many parents want to monitor what their children can access. To help parents, ratings systems, warning labels, and electronic blocking devices have been created. These are designed to tell parents which products contain excessive violence or sex. These warnings can also help you make informed decisions about products you may want to avoid. For some people, warning labels and devices are helpful; others see them as a form of censorship because someone else has judged the content.

People have strong opinions about media violence, both for and against. It's an emotional topic because violence affects many lives today. Media violence is often criticized for influencing people to commit real-life violence. Teens need to be aware of the effects of media violence. Every day, you are confronted by the media. Every time you turn on the television, listen to the radio, or go to the movies, you are being influenced by the media. But you also have power based on the decisions you make when you buy, or don't buy, their products. By being more aware of media violence, you will be able to use your power as a consumer to make a difference.

The media has the power to reach millions of people through many different formats.

Chapter 1

Understanding the Media

Today, the media play an important role in society. Many newspapers, magazines, radio and television stations, movies, and web sites exist. The media inform, instruct, and entertain. They present information on factual matters ranging from crime, political issues, and financial data, to weather reports, school closings, and movie listings. They present fictional stories in articles, movies, and television programs.

In the past, the media were not as visible in daily life. Before radio gained popularity in the 1920s and television in the 1940s, people got their news through newspapers or word of mouth. Many people lived in remote areas and didn't receive current news for days. When news finally arrived, it was often a month or more old.

Now life is fast paced and people expect instant service, whether it's from hamburger joints or from news crews. When O. J. Simpson was suspected of murdering his ex-wife, Nicole Brown Simpson, and her friend Ronald Goldman, and fled police, reporters followed the event and brought coverage into homes throughout the world. When Israeli Prime Minister Yitzhak Rabin was assassinated or when terrorists bombed a federal building in Oklahoma, radio and television stations interrupted their usual coverage to bring lengthy reports about these events, often before all the facts were known. When Princess Diana died, the whole world witnessed her funeral as it was happening.

What Drives the Media?

When an unusual event occurs, movie producers, television executives, and book publishers compete to obtain permission from those involved to tell their stories first. All forms of the media want to be the first to present the story. Often, inaccurate information is the result. Why all the frenzy? Money.

Money drives the media. Like any industry, the media are in business to make a profit. Radio, television, newspapers, and magazines rely on advertising to finance their operations. Companies buy air time to promote their products via commercials on television and radio; they buy space for advertisements in newspapers and magazines. Films are financed by producers who expect to make money from ticket and later video sales. Record companies also expect profits from sales. All media create products that people "buy," whether you actually

Buying a product tells the media that you like what they show, print, and broadcast.

purchase a video, CD, or newspaper, tune into a radio or television program, or pay to see a film. You're telling advertisers and producers that you like their products and are willing to spend money for them.

If stories don't sell well, they won't be told. Companies pay a lot of money to advertise their products. So if people aren't tuning into that station, reading that magazine, or seeing that movie, advertisers will look for one that does attract consumers. There is stiff competition in the media to capture advertising and consumer dollars.

Today, people have access to many information sources. So the media compete to find stories that they think are the most interesting or unusual. When they are the first on the scene or the first with a movie, television show, or book about an event or subject, the producer gains an edge over the competition. When the media attract more consumers, more companies want to advertise with them.

Understanding what drives or motivates the media is essential to understanding media violence. The media try to present interesting and unusual topics to draw larger audiences and make more money. They often look for more and more shocking tales to tell because they think people are tired of hearing the same stories everyday. Many people have become desensitized to violent stories. As a result, the media search for tales of more unusual acts—stories that will interest audiences. Often, those shocking tales involve excessive violence.

Whether it's true-life killers like Ted Bundy or Jack the Ripper, or fictional villains like *Friday the 13th*'s Jason or *Nightmare on Elm Street*'s Freddy Krueger, violence makes money for the media because people are frightened, yet fascinated by it. Many people have shown that they will pay to see violence.

It is important to remember that the media present stories with excessive violence because these stories are unusual. These tales are not about average people. Also, many violent films and television shows are not based on reality and do not show an honest picture of everyday life. Just because a frightening event receives a lot of news coverage doesn't mean it happens a lot.

Chapter 2

Violence on Film

Some of the earliest films showed shocking acts of violence. The silent picture *Birth of a Nation* (1915) featured battle scenes from the American Civil War and violence by the Ku Klux Klan. While these scenes may seem tame to today's moviegoers, they were terrifying at that time. Many early films didn't show excessive blood and gore. If people were shot, they fell down without spurts of blood coming from their wounds. In the 1960s, however, some directors decided to show violence in a more realistic way.

In *Psycho* (1960), a maniac stabs a woman as she showers. Filmed in black and white, the scene depicts her murder, although viewers never see her stabbed. The scene switches between pictures of a raised knife, the woman's stomach, the woman's face, and blood washing down the drain. Viewers never saw the knife

This shower scene from *Psycho* shocked audiences who weren't used to seeing violent acts on the big screen.

enter her body. However, the violence was chilling and shocked audiences.

Other filmmakers also began to use more graphic violence in movies, including *Bonnie & Clyde* (1967) and *The Wild Bunch* (1969). In these movies, both about bank robbers, excessive violence was shown in slow motion to increase the impact of the violence on audiences. Bullets ripped into the chests of victims; blood spurted from their bodies.

In the movie *In Cold Blood* (1967), viewers were shocked to see a fictionalized account of the true-life murder of a farm family. Such acts were uncommon at that time. Today, however, random murders are more frequent and often are featured in movie plots, including those aimed at teenage audiences. When *In Cold Blood* was remade as a television movie in 1996, the story wasn't nearly as shocking as it had been thirty years earlier.

Types of Film Violence

Violence on film is presented in several ways. There is true-to-life violence that shows viewers what typically happens when violence occurs. For example, in a fistfight, a man can get knocked out; if pushed down stairs, a woman may break a leg; if gangs clash, someone may die.

Cartoon violence is a type commonly found in animated programs. In cartoons, a coyote may accidentally blow himself up trying to catch a roadrunner, then shake it off and try again. The real results of shootings, fights, and falls aren't shown in movies featuring cartoon violence. Some cartoons, like those included in *Spike and Mike's Sick and Twisted Animation Festival,* glorify violence, and present it in a way that is supposed to be funny. Cartoon violence is used in both animated and nonanimated movies. When the media use cartoon violence, the victim doesn't feel the consequences for very long, if at all. In movies, characters may be severely beaten, shot at hundreds of times, buried alive, or left for dead in an explosion, all without serious emotional or physical injury.

Home Alone (1990), a nonanimated film, used cartoon violence. In one scene, the movie's hero defends his home against burglars by rigging a hot iron to hit one of the robbers in the face. The burglar is stunned for a moment, then continues.

Another type of violence is found in horror films. The violence in horror movies is meant to shock viewers and is extremely graphic. Gruesome beheadings, severed limbs, and chainsaw murders are common. Horror fans like gore because of the special effects used to create it. Villains in these movies are always difficult or impossible to kill.

Martial arts or ninja movies feature a lot of violence, particularly kicks to someone's head and chest. The violence is performed by skilled professionals and the fight scenes are usually choreographed—designed and rehearsed in advance. Villains and heroes suffer repeatedly, usually without much lasting damage to their bodies.

Home Alone is one of the most popular movies of all time. Its use of cartoon violence made audiences laugh.

What Violence Says or Doesn't Say

Filmmakers are often criticized because there is so much violence in movies. Some people aren't bothered by it, but many are very concerned. Movies show scenes that are much more violent than those on network television, although many movies later appear unedited on cable television.

A movie like *Pulp Fiction* illustrates the controversy about film violence. The movie uses gratuitous violence. One scene shows a drug dealer shooting a teenager by mistake in a car. The boy's brain splatters against the rear windshield and back onto the dealers. The shooter apologizes for the mess, therefore mixing violence with humor.

The scene is gratuitous because: 1) the shooting is exceptionally gory; 2) the scene that follows includes dialogue that is supposed to be funny; and 3) the violence was used for shock value. Some people refused to see the movie; others walked out of the theater. However, the movie received positive reviews and was nominated for film awards. *Pulp Fiction* shows how differently people respond to media violence.

Movies with gratuitous violence often gloss over the consequences of violence. Where do all the bullets land in a shoot-out on a crowded street? If a cop uses excessive force to stop criminals and doesn't call for help, is he a hero, a vigilante (someone who takes the law into his own hands), or should he be punished for abusing his power? If someone shoots a store owner, how does

Pulp Fiction presented violence in a cool, hip way, provoking mixed reactions from filmgoers.

the killer feel once he's in prison? How does the family of the store owner feel? Action movies, in particular, show a lot of gratuitous violence without depicting the consequences. Rarely do action movies show families realistically mourning over the deceased, especially if he or she was a criminal. Also, movies rarely show how a killer feels after committing the act of murder.

Warnings About Violent Content

To ease concerns about content, the Motion Picture Association of America (MPAA) began rating movies in 1968. Under the system, movies are rated based on the amount of sexual content, violence, and adult content. The ratings are:

- **G**- General audiences. Movies with little or no sex and violence.
- **PG**- Parental guidance suggested for children. Movies with mild sex and violence.
- **PG13**- Parental guidance suggested for children under thirteen. Movies with profanity (strong language) and a higher degree of sex and violence.
- **R**- Restricted; no one under seventeen admitted without a parent. Movies with adult themes, profanity, graphic sex, and violence.
- **NC17**- No one under seventeen admitted. Movies with strong adult themes, profanity, excessive nudity, sex, and violence.

The ratings system is designed to help parents decide what movies may be inappropriate for their children. Ratings can also help teens make informed decisions about movies. People who support ratings do so because the ratings give people information about a movie's content. Opponents believe that ratings are too subjective—or based on someone else's opinion. They believe people mature differently, and ratings may not be accurate for everyone. Opponents see ratings as a form of censorship because some people will decide not to see a movie because of its rating. What do you think about the ratings system? Does it help you by limiting the amount of violence you see, or is it too restrictive?

Chapter 3

Violence on Television

Early network television didn't include a lot of violence. (Network television includes stations that broadcast over public airwaves—ABC, CBS, FOX, NBC, and PBS.) Network programs are monitored by censors hired by the industry. These censors view programs for sex, violence, and offensive language, and inform producers if the content is too strong. For example, when *I Love Lucy* aired in the 1950s, Lucy could not use the word "pregnant," even though she was. Over time, censors have changed their standards, so shows now use words that were once banned from television.

Censors have also allowed more violence and sex to be shown on television. In the 1970s and 1980s, violence became increasingly popular on evening dramas. Producers said it was more realistic and people wanted to see it. Shoot-outs between heroes and criminals were

Words and actions once banned on TV shows, such as *I Love Lucy*, are commonplace today.

frequent on shows. Rarely were the heroes hit or hurt despite numerous attempts on their lives. The heroes narrowly escaped death every week and went on to face new villains.

In such shows, television presented amazing heroes with unusual luck. Viewers watched these shows because they were about incredible characters—not average people like themselves.

Easy Access to Violence

Amazing heroes are still popular today. And violence can be found in almost every type of television show—dramas, sitcoms, music videos, sports events, talk shows, news programs, science fiction/fantasy programs, real-life shows, comedy routines, cartoons, and movies. Television violence causes great concern because television is so easily accessible: You just flick a switch on your TV set and it's in your home. Most American homes have at least one television set.

To see how much violence is televised, let's look at some examples.

Dramas

Some dramas are based on real-life violence, including *Law and Order* and *Homicide: Life on the Street.* These programs deal well with violence because they examine the consequences as well as the act.

Other dramas, such as *Beverly Hills 90210* and the Canadian show *North of Sixty*, aren't based on violence but sometimes deal with violent situations. In *Beverly Hills 90210*, the character, Kelly, was the victim of a drive-by shooting. The show effectively dealt with the effects of the shooting on her life and those around her. In *North of Sixty*, a show about Native Americans and others in a small town, teens sometimes resort to violence but always learn from it.

Sitcoms (Situation Comedies)

On occasion, sitcoms discuss violence. However, sitcoms present most subjects in a shallow way. This happens because sitcoms have a half hour (minus the time used for commercials) to present and resolve a conflict. Humor is used to lessen the effect of any problem faced

An early Star Trek episode shows violence in a futuristic world.

by the characters. So, if a bully takes a kid's money, the problem is always resolved by the end of the show. Yet real people, when bullied, usually don't laugh about it and can't resolve their problems so quickly.

Fantasy/Science Fiction

Fantasy programs include shows like *Xena: Warrior Princess, Hercules: The Legendary Journeys, Highlander,* and *The Mighty Morphin Power Rangers.* In these stories, heroes constantly fight to save the world from evil. The violence in these shows doesn't seem real because the programs are meant to be a fantasy. The same is true with science fiction shows such as *Star Trek* and *Babylon 5.* Space adventurers travel the galaxies and sometimes battle with those who are out to destroy other worlds and life forms. *The X-Files* combines science fiction with contemporary life as FBI agents investigate unexplained phenomena. Violence is often portrayed as the agents try to stop criminals and alien beings.

Real-Life Shows

These shows are very popular. Viewers watch *COPS, America's Most Wanted,* and *Real Stories of the Highway Patrol* to see doors busted down, car chases, criminals arrested, and sometimes real (not staged) violence.

Other programs are devoted to real animal attacks and show wild animals attacking other species, including humans. People capture these events on video cameras and show them on television. The attacks are violent and gory, and used to shock people.

Court proceedings are also popular, especially when they deal with violent acts. During O. J. Simpson's double-murder trial, cameras were allowed inside the courtroom. The case was televised worldwide. Many people believe the television cameras influenced the trial—and turned it into entertainment. Viewers wondered if the lawyers, judge, and witnesses were putting on a show for the cameras. As a result, Simpson's later civil trial was not televised. The juries in both trials reached different verdicts about Simpson's involvement in the murder.

Music Videos

Some music videos feature violence because of the

themes in the songs. Guns, drugs, murder, and hate—
all are depicted in a flurry of images. Rap, heavy metal,
and punk rock videos are often criticized for encourag-
ing and glamorizing violence. Musicians defend the
depiction of violence, saying it reflects real life on the
street.

Talk Shows

Many talk shows also cover violent topics. Subjects range
from "My Man Beats Me But I Still Love Him" to "Neo-
Nazi Skinheads: Are They Taking Over Your
Neighborhood?" These shows often feature guests who
brag about their violent acts while the audience boos.
Some guests threaten or scream at audience members or
other participants and even resort to violence on stage.

When a young man was killed after the taping of a
Jenny Jones show, in which he revealed a crush on another man, many people began to question the format and
subject matter of daytime talk shows. This violent episode
was a wake-up call to the people who produce and watch
the shows.

Many viewers have grown tired of these shows and call
them "trash talk." Shows with positive and upbeat themes,
like *The Oprah Winfrey Show* and *The Rosie O'Donnell
Show*, have gained more popularity and respect.

Sports

Sports are often violent. Hockey players fight on the
ice. Baseball players run onto the field when a pitcher

hits a batter. Many sports stars, often considered heroes because of their skill, display violent behavior. For example, basketball player Dennis Rodman was suspended for eleven games after kicking a cameraman in 1997, and Mike Tyson was fined $3 million after he bit the ear of his opponent, Evander Holyfield, during a boxing match for the Heavyweight Championship.

News

Violent stories are usually presented first on newscasts. Not only do you hear about violence in your town, but from around the world as well. For a detailed discussion of news, see Chapter Four.

Cartoons

Cartoons have been violent for years. Popeye battled Bluto and Elmer Fudd hunted Bugs Bunny. Violence was and continues to be essential to these stories. Today's cartoons are more graphic and less humorous, while the villains are more evil. Cartoons like *The Teenage Mutant Ninja Turtles, Ren and Stimpy,* and *Beavis and Butt-Head* have raised concern because some children try to imitate the violence depicted in these shows.

Movies

Films that are first shown in theaters are often partially edited for profanity, violence, and sex for network television. Some movies made for network television

In cartoons such as *The Teenage Mutant Ninja Turtles*, violence has increased significantly in recent years.

also feature violent content that must be approved by the station's censors.

Cable Television
While network television is criticized for its portrayal of violence, people are also concerned about graphic material shown on cable channels. For a small fee, viewers can subscribe to cable and see movies from the theater, unedited. Some parents worry that while they are away at work their children will watch these movies.

Warnings About Violent Content
Some people have urged the government to reduce the amount of television violence. Instead, the television

industry decided to create a ratings system much like the movie rating system. TV ratings are shown in the upper left-hand corner of programs as they begin. They are also included in television guides. Sports and news programs are not rated, however. Ratings include:

- TV-Y   Children of all ages.
- TV-Y7   Children seven and older. Program may contain mild violence.
- TV-G   General audiences. Program may contain little or no sex, violence, and profanity.
- TV-PG   Parental guidance advised for children. Program has some mild sex, violence, and profanity.
- TV-14   Parental guidance advised for children under fourteen. Program has a higher degree of sex, violence, and profanity.
- TV-M   Mature audiences. Programs may contain graphic violence, sex, and profanity, and may not be appropriate for teens under seventeen.

Also included are the following labels:

D	suggestive dialogue
L	coarse language
S	sex
V	violence
FV	fantasy violence

Ratings are designed to help people decide what to watch, particularly parents who want to monitor what their children view. Ratings alert people to the content

CHANNEL

Parental Control
Signal Type
Signal Source
Lists and Labels
Auto Channel Searc
Auto Tuning
Video 1 Input Sour

Concerned parents can use blocking devices to prevent their children from watching certain shows.

of a show before they decide to watch it. Some people claim that ratings are too subjective and act as censorship. Others think the ratings don't provide enough detailed information on a show's content.

Cable's pay channels have offered more complete information about programs, particularly movies. Before a movie begins, its MPAA rating is given, followed by whether the show contains graphic violence, strong sexual content, and profanity. Some network shows, like ABC's *NYPD Blue*, have carried warnings about nudity and violence. They were added because of the show's controversial nature. Some local stations refused to show the program, while some advertisers withdrew their commercials and therefore their advertising dollars. The show's additional warnings were added to appease some viewers and advertisers.

The V-Chip

In addition to television ratings, it is a federal law that an electronic device called the V-Chip must be built into new television sets beginning in February, 1998. The V-Chip can be programmed to block out shows with high ratings of sex and violence.

The V-Chip is designed to help parents monitor what their children watch. It is also controversial. Supporters of the V-Chip believe it makes people more aware of the content of television shows. They also think it helps parents ensure their children are watching shows appropriate for their age.

Opponents of the V-Chip say that teens know more about technology than their parents and can reprogram the V-Chip without anyone knowing. Others complain that the V-Chip won't help reduce the amount of violence on television. Also, most homes won't have V-Chip televisions for years because it's too costly to buy new television sets.

Chapter 4

Violence in the News

The news—whether printed, online, or broadcast on television or radio—is full of violence. Just pick up any newspaper or tune into any news program. You'll learn what horrible acts have occurred worldwide. "If it bleeds, it leads"—this saying shows the importance that the news media place on stories that include violence and explains that the news media lead off their programs with violent stories because they are shocking or different. Reporters hope to gain people's attention because they want more people to read or watch their news program. This means more advertising dollars for them.

New Technology

The amount of violence in the news today is much higher than in the past. Before television and radio, people

News reporters are very aggressive in pursuing stories that will attract viewers.

received reports through newspapers or word of mouth. News reporting changes as new technologies become available and the speed of news delivery has rapidly increased. During World War II (1939-1945), reports were given on radio. Filmed news reports, called news-reels, were shown at movie theaters. During the U.S. involvement in the Vietnam War, which began in the late 1960s, news crews brought stories and pictures of the war into people's homes on television. Through tele-vision, people of all ages and backgrounds saw the hor-rors of war for the first time.

The use of satellites today allows the news media to report on events as they happen worldwide . People not only learn about violence in their communities, but acts committed far away. In 1991 television viewers watched as Iraq was bombed during the Persian Gulf War. You can't read a newspaper or tune into a news program without hearing about violence—and lots of it. Because reporters deliver the news so fast, people rely on it for information about everything.

Placing Importance on a Story

The news media can affect the importance that people place on events. The O. J. Simpson trial is a good exam-ple. Murders occur every day. But in this case the accused murderer was a former sports star suspected of killing his ex-wife (who was of a different race) along with her male companion. These factors made the story unusual. News crews provided excessive coverage of the double

Every day, millions of viewers tuned in to see the latest events unfolding at O. J. Simpson's murder trial.

murder. Reporters made people feel that the outcome of the trial was of vital importance to them. While it is important to prosecute murder suspects, many people are killed without receiving any attention from the news media. The same is true of the murder of six-year-old beauty queen JonBenet Ramsey. How many young children are murdered every day without capturing the media's attention? Is one person's life more important than another?

We can explore this question by looking at how the media covered the deaths of Princess Diana and Mother Theresa. Some feel the news gave more coverage to Princess Diana's death because of her celebrity status and the violent way in which she died. Many stations' coverage of the funeral exceeded ten continuous hours. Mother Theresa, who dedicated her life to helping others and was considered by many to be a living saint, was not given equal coverage. Did the media act responsibly when they covered these two stories?

The media emphasize stories like these because they are unusual and attract viewers and readers. However, most people feel the media focus too much attention on events like these, and often put less effort into stories that are of greater importance to more people.

Irresponsible Reporting

News reports may also lead people to misread situations. The case of Richard Jewell is a good example. Jewell was suspected of bombing Olympic Park in Atlanta during the 1996 Olympics. Many news crews were in Atlanta to cover the Olympics, so when the bomb exploded, reporters raced to the scene. Stories were written about Jewell's involvement and his photo appeared on television, in newspapers, and on the Internet.

In the United States, a person is considered innocent until proven guilty in court. However, many reporters assumed Jewell was guilty because he was being questioned by authorities. People thought he was guilty, too, because of the news reports. Jewell, however, never went to trial. Authorities couldn't find any evidence that showed he was involved in the bombing. Richard Jewell was cleared and the news media reported that fact, but

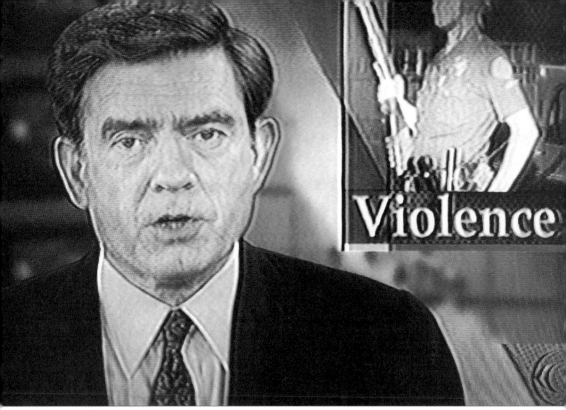

When the news focuses on violent stories, many people begin to believe that violence is more common than it really is.

the damage was done. Once something is reported, many people tend to believe it. Even though a mistake was made, some people will always associate Jewell with the 1996 Olympics bombing. Jewell's life has greatly suffered because of irresponsible reporting.

Can the Media Encourage Violence?

The attention given to some violent news stories can also lead to more violence, and reporters capture that additional violence as well. The case of Rodney King shows how this can happen. King, a black man, was beaten by white Los Angeles police officers during an arrest. The beating was filmed by an onlooker and then shown on newscasts worldwide. People were outraged to see the police beating someone. Some of the police officers were tried in court and not convicted. Witnesses said that the news did not broadcast the whole video. They claimed that King had resisted arrest and that police were trying to subdue him. Many others felt that no one should be beaten like that even if he had resisted arrest. When the police were not convicted, race riots broke out in Los Angeles. Many people were killed, hurt, or robbed during the riots.

Did the excessive news coverage of the King beating and trials fuel the subsequent riots? If people hadn't seen the video of the beating over and over again, would they have been compelled to commit such violence in return? Had the news shown the whole video, would the reaction have been the same? While the public has a right to know about police brutality, the media can distort an event based on the information they choose to give you—and how much of it they give you. The media often doesn't inform people on how they can work in peaceful ways to end police brutality or other injustices.

"Breaking" a Story

The news media always look for an unusual angle to a story. They want to be first on the scene to report, or "break," the story. Many television news crews cut into other programs to bring viewers a "breaking" story— one that has just happened or is still occurring, such as a hostage situation, a plane crash, or an assassination. Journalists look for witnesses who will give information to their newspaper or station first. This is called an exclusive. An exclusive means that the reporter is the only one who has that specific information at that time. Being first with exclusive information attracts more viewers and, in turn, more advertising dollars. How many times have you heard news anchors say, "Channel 7 was first on the scene," or "Channel 4 has the exclusive at 11:00"?

Since there are many news sources, journalists need to make their stories stand out. Sometimes they interview people at crime and accident scenes. Reporters may ask witnesses to describe what they saw, ask survivors how they feel, or ask relatives and friends to describe the person who died. Often, reporters show people crying or very upset. Do journalists really need to interview people in their time of grief? Would you want to be interviewed right after you found out about someone's death?

Chapter 5

Violence in Other Media

Other media are criticized for violent content, too. This chapter looks at violence on the radio and on the Internet.

Radio

Before television, people listened to their favorite dramas on the radio. Some had violent themes. One production, in particular, shows the influence of radio at that time. It was the 1938 broadcast of *The War of the Worlds* performed by Orson Welles and the Mercury Theatre. In an attempt to draw listeners, the cast made the play as realistic as possible. They used fictional news reports to tell a story about Martians overtaking Earth, including descriptions of the violence used. Although the cast told its listeners it was fiction, many people believed the takeover was really happening and

Even though it is not a visual medium, the radio can influence its listeners with the type of music that is played and stories that are broadcast.

panicked. Some tried to flee cities by car; others prepared to die. Although people were mad at Welles for the misunderstanding, he gained more listeners because of it.

The Federal Communications Commission (FCC) was established in 1934 by the U.S. Government. The commission regulates radio and television in the public interest. This means they make sure these industries are serving the public. In 1991, the FCC set limits for advertising during children's programs. It can also renew or revoke a stations broadcasting license, or fine a station for using offensive language.

Radio continues to attract listeners. It provides the latest news, popular music, and talk shows that discuss important issues. Violence is often described in each of these areas. Although listeners have to picture the descriptions in their minds, some depictions are so vivid that little is left to the imagination.

Radio talk shows receive the same criticisms as television talk shows. People complain that some shows give violent or rude people a chance to brag about their hurtful behaviors. Some listeners think talk programs allow hate groups to spread spiteful messages.

Music

Violence is also described in music, particularly gangsta rap, heavy metal, and punk rock. For example, rap artists take a lot of criticism for songs about violence. Some people believe the songs glorify murder, guns, drugs, and violence against women. When rapper Tupak Shakur was murdered, some claimed his death was the result of the violence that filled his music.

Heavy metal bands are criticized for violence in their lyrics as well. Some people think these musicians also advocate sexual violence against women. Some teens admit they have attempted suicide or murder after listening to some violent songs. The band Judas Priest was accused of inspiring a teen to commit suicide. On occasion, songs reflect the musicians' violent actions in concert, whether it's biting off bats' heads, smashing guitars on stage, or stabbing their keyboards. The band, Marilyn Manson, has been banned from playing concerts in certain cities because of their violent stageshow.

Warnings About Violent Content

People, particularly parents, are concerned about violence in music. Some groups, such as the Parent's Music Resource Center (PMRC) led by Tipper Gore—wife of U.S. Vice President Al Gore—have worked to make more information available to music buyers. In 1990 warning labels first appeared on music products that contained strong profanity or violent content. These labels say "Parental Advisory: Explicit Lyrics" and are placed on the covers of compact discs, cassettes, and music videos.

Supporters of warning labels believe that the stickers provide people with more information about the product. They say the labels are extremely important because of the amount of graphic violence and sex in some musicians' lyrics. Opponents of the labels believe they are a form of censorship, because someone else has decided what is too sexual or violent. They believe that the stickers impact an artist's creativity because department stores may refuse to sell items carrying warning labels. Others suggest that labels encourage sales because they provoke curiosity. Some teens may buy these products to rebel against their parents.

The Internet

Violence is also found on the Internet. This issue received much attention when a college student was questioned by police about a story he wrote that appeared on the Internet. His fictional account

The Internet is a regular part of many teens' lives, but parents and lawmakers are having trouble regulating it because it is so accessible.

described the rape of another student—a young woman who strongly resembled one of his classmates.

The accessibility of violence on the Internet has some people worried that teens or young children might access one of these web sites by surfing (randomly searching) the Net. Because of this, many online services provide software that prevents people from entering these sites by mistake, and the programs are designed for parents who want their children to avoid these sites. However, many teens are computer literate and can dismantle the software.

When using the Internet, you need to be careful about how much information you give out about yourself, especially in chat rooms and on e-mail. Since you don't often know who you are contacting, proceed with caution. If someone sends you a violent, vulgar, or offensive message, don't respond to it. Tell your parents about it. And don't send messages like that yourself— you could put yourself in danger and your service provider may cancel your account.

Since the Internet is a relatively new medium, many lawmakers are unsure of how to regulate it and how to enforce any laws they might pass. The Internet is a difficult medium to police because it is so large and spreads worldwide. Many believe any restriction would be a violation of their First Amendment rights.

Chapter 6

Effects of Media Violence

*M*ichael and Antonio left the movie theater. Michael couldn't stop thinking about the movie on the way home. "I loved the part when Bruce took those guys out. Yeah, you mess with Bruce and you pay," Michael said. "I should lay it out for Laurence like that. He's been hanging around Carla."

"You want to get even with Laurence?" Antonio asked. "Just because Bruce didn't go to jail for beating that guy doesn't mean you won't. It was a movie, Mike. You won't impress Carla with violence."

Media violence does affect people. Studies show that by age eighteen, teens will see between 16,000 and 25,000 murders on television. But media violence affects people differently. Some of its effects include:

- **Disrespect/Cynicism:** A study by the American Medical Association (AMA) in 1996 stated that one of the biggest problems with media violence is that it causes people to be disrespectful of others. When people use violence, they are showing that disrespect. In the worst case, a lack of respect for human life can lead to murder.

- **Desensitization:** When people see so much violence, some begin to think it is common or acceptable behavior. Eventually people become desensitized to it and may become less outraged when they are exposed to it, including the violence that may impact their own lives. They may actually expect life situations to be violent. Some people no longer get upset or are shocked about violence, feeling that it is inevitable.

- **Aggressive Behavior:** Most people are exposed to media violence during childhood. Studies show that teens and young children tend to be more aggressive when they have been exposed to media violence over a long period of time. As a result, they may respond violently to some situations. Children who are just learning how to behave, may have a hard time seeing the difference between cartoon violence and real violence. As a result, they may act overly aggressive.

- **Fear:** Media violence can cause fear in some people. These people may start to worry that violence is more common than it really is. This feeling can occur because violence is found in nearly every form of

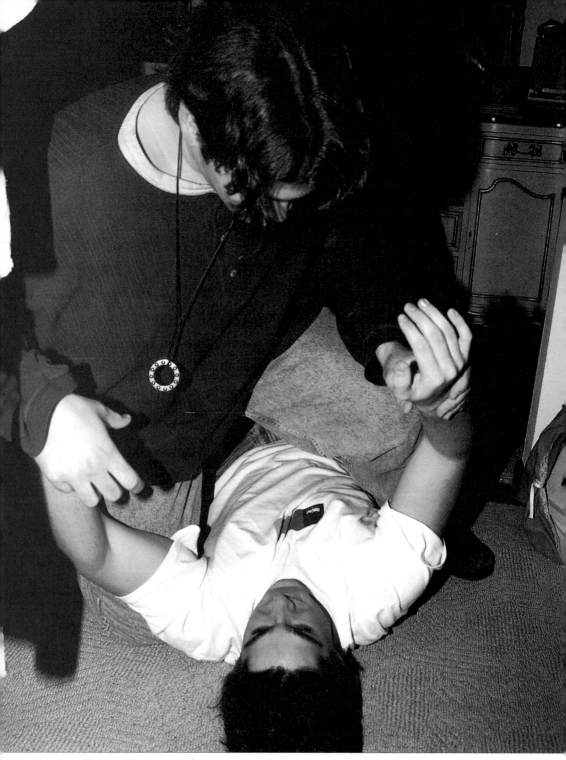

Researchers conduct many studies in an attempt to explore the connection between media violence and real-life aggression.

entertainment—including some not discussed in this book, like comic books, graphic novels, and video games.

• **Imitation:** Some try to imitate what they see in the media. This happened after the movie *Money Train* opened in 1995. In the film, a madman sets a subway token booth on fire and the clerk barely escapes. When a real subway token booth was torched after the movie debuted, the clerk died. A similar situation occurred after a fire was set on the *Beavis and Butt-Head* cartoon. After watching the program, a little boy started a fire. His sister died. Luckily, most people, however, don't imitate media violence to that degree.

• **Wanting More:** Some people are thrilled by violence and want to see and hear more about it.

Media Violence Is Misleading

Media violence is often misleading. In many instances, the consequences of violence aren't shown. While you are shown massive amounts of blood and gore, you often don't see what happens to the criminal after he's arrested. For example, what happens to him in prison? Does he become a victim of prison violence? Does he have nightmares about what he did? When someone resorts to violence to end a conflict, does the problem really end or does a new one begin?

The media send a mixed message when heroes use violence. For example, people expect villains to be violent and it's easy to dislike them when they hurt people. But when heroes use violence, are the media saying it is okay to use violence to stop bad people? Are heroes justified in using it?

The media tell powerful stories. When you see a hero fight a villain onscreen, you may feel like you want to help. Do you feel relief when the villain is hurt or killed? Do you applaud? Do you feel any sadness that a life was taken? Despite what the media lead you to believe, violence is never a good solution to a problem. If everyone used violence to end conflict, our hospitals and cemeteries would be even more crowded than they are today.

The media also send mixed messages when violent people are portrayed as cool. Most violent people end up in prison or dead. Hollywood often presents criminals who are attractive, smart, witty, and likable. Sometimes audiences are encouraged to like the criminals more than the police who are trying to stop them. Hollywood often presents cops who are stupid, clumsy, or corrupt. Are criminals really that smart and charming?

Violence is also misleading when it is combined with humor. What is funny about violence? Many people who have experienced the death of a loved one aren't amused when audiences are made to laugh when someone dies. Violence mixed with humor is most often found in programs featuring cartoon violence. Since cartoon violence doesn't seem real, audiences may find it acceptable to laugh.

Stereotyping

Media violence also encourages negative stereotypes about people. Stereotypes are characteristics that people generally associate with a certain group of people.

To see how stereotypes are used in the media, take the following quiz: 1) How many movies feature Arabs as terrorists? (Hint: *True Lies* and *Executive Decision* are just two.) 2) Name five movies with Arab heroes. 3) How many Hispanic Americans play leading roles on television series, and how many are shown in small roles as criminals? 4) Name programs in the last two years that have featured modern-day Native Americans in positive roles. 5) In the last year, how many women in movies couldn't defend themselves? 6) When strong women are depicted in movies, are they also villains?

The answers to these questions will be different for everyone. However, they point out two problems in how violence is depicted. First, many ethnic groups are stereotyped into negative and violent roles and are rarely shown in positive roles. Second, there aren't many roles available to minority groups at all. In the past the film industry used Italians to portray Native Americans. In recent years, this has changed and Native Americans are finally being cast in movies that portray their people.

It is important to remember that the media often do not represent people fairly or truthfully and use stereotypes when presenting violence. Unfortunately, the media frequently use the stereotypes discussed above, and these negative characteristics are reinforced in people's minds. Some people accept stereotypes and don't learn the truth for themselves. This leads one to wonder: Would people of different races fear each other if the media didn't show so many whites as racists and so many blacks as criminals? Would a movie be just as exciting if these stereotypes were broken? It may take some time before we find out. But progress has been made. Before *Xena: Warrior Princess*, all the strong, action heroes on television were men. Before *Ellen,* there were no gay or lesbian actors starring in their own sitcoms. Using your power as a media activist may pave the way for more changes.

Chapter 7

What You Can Do

K*elsey was disappointed after watching the new show. She had waited for weeks to see it. The program was too violent and the characters were too evil. She had hoped it would be better. Her sister, Sarah, didn't like how much violence she saw on television. She had written a letter to the network complaining about it. Kelsey thought about writing a letter, too, but she was concerned about the issue of censorship. "If I tell others not to watch it, then I'm deciding what they should or shouldn't watch," Kelsey thought. "But if we can discuss it in class, I can explain why I thought the program was too violent and see how others feel."*

If you are concerned about media violence or the issue of censorship, there are various organizations you can join. (See the Where to Go for Help section for some

Writing letters to TV networks, newspapers, or film companies
is a great way to tell them what you think of their products.

ideas.) Regardless of where you stand on the issue, it is important for you to become media literate. You need to understand what is being presented and why. Don't forget that the media are in business to make money. They will only make those products that sell well. To learn more about media literacy, contact an organization like the Center for Media Education or the Center for Media Literacy.

Here are some other tips:

• Be selective in the media products you buy. When you buy violent products, you send the message that you like or accept violence and will pay for it.

• Treat the media like strangers. Don't accept everything they tell you. Think for yourself. Would you listen to strangers you met on the street talk on and on about sex and violence? Don't be fooled into believing things that you know just can't be true. The media aren't always right.

• Walk away from products that offend you. Don't lie to your friends about liking something just so they think you're cool. Chances are they were offended too but are afraid to say so.

• Choose your heroes carefully. Just because someone is skilled in sports or is a good musician doesn't mean he or she is a hero. Admire people who resolve conflict without violence, rather than the ones who do.

• Write to producers, directors, writers, and advertisers if you're really offended by their products or write to the FCC.

- Ask your school to sponsor discussions about media violence. Does your school have a Students Against Violence program or something similar? Such programs encourage teens to avoid using violence like they see in the media.
- Encourage discussions with your friends. Share information.
- Ask television and radio stations to address issues with call-in programs.
- Urge the media to participate in antiviolence campaigns.
- Mentor others about alternative solutions to violence. Help them become media literate.
- Be selective in channel surfing. Don't watch something just because nothing else is on that interests you. Instead read a book or volunteer with school, church, or community projects.
- Try watching public television (PBS) or listening to public radio (NPR). These stations are funded by viewer contributions and private donations, so they don't need to compete for advertising dollars.
- Talk to your parents or an adult when you see something that bothers you. If your parents forbid you to watch a show or see a movie, ask why. If you really want to see it, explain why and suggest you watch it together.

Glossary

activist To support or oppose a controversial issue by taking action.

cartoon violence Violence that is used in cartoons, comedies, or action movies that isn't realistic because the victim doesn't feel the consequences for very long, if at all.

censorship Removing or editing content that some people may find offensive.

choreograph To plan out and rehearse in advance, such as a dance routine or a fight sequence.

contempt Strong dislike and disrespect for someone or something.

cynicism Believing that people are motivated by their own self-interest.

desensitize Seeing something so often you stop being shocked by it and stop caring about it.

disrespect Not valuing something or not treating it with respect.

glamorize To make something seem attractive and cool.

glorify To make something seem better than it really is.

graphic Clearly shown; vivid.

gratuitous Excessive, needless, and pointless.

media Information providers, such as television, radio, newspapers, movies or the Internet.

profanity Strong, foul, or offensive language.

rating systems Coding that rates programs based on the degree of sex, violence, and profanity in them.

realism The attempt to show things as they really are.

satellite An man-made object that orbits around Earth and is used to send weather and other scientific information back to Earth; it also transmits television shows across earth.

stereotypes Mostly negative characteristics given to people of different ethnic, social, or economic backgrounds by others who don't know them.

terrorists People who use violence against innocent victims to make their causes known.

V-Chip Device installed on new television sets that, when programmed, blocks out shows containing a high degree of sex and violence.

vigilante Someone who seeks justice on his own, rather than waiting for police.

Where to Go for Help

Center for Media Education
1511 K Street, N.W., Suite 518
Washington, DC 20005
(202) 628-2620
Web site: http://tap.epn.org/cme

Center for Media Literacy
4727 Wilshire Boulevard, Suite 403
Los Angeles, CA 90010
(213) 931-4177
Web site: http://www.medialit.org

Federal Communications Commission (FCC)
1919 M Street, N.W.
Washington, DC 20554
(202) 418-0200
Web site: http://www.fcc.gov

The Freedom Forum World Center
1101 Wilson Boulevard
Arlington, VA 22209
(703) 528-0800
Web site: http://www.freedomforum.org

In Canada:

Canadians Concerned About Violence in Entertainment (C-CAVE)
167 Glen Road
Toronto, Ontario, M4W 2W8 Canada
(416) 961-0853

For Further Reading

Beyond Blame: Challenging Violence in the Media. Los Angeles, CA: Center for Media Literacy, 1996.

Day, Nancy. *Violence in Schools.* Springfield, NJ: Enslow Publishers, Inc., 1996.

Kohn, Martin F. *VideoHound's Family Video Guide.* Detroit, MI: Visible Ink Press, 1997.

Lewis, Barbara A. *The Kid's Guide to Social Action: How to Solve the Social Problems You Choose— and Turn Creative Thinking into Positive Action.* Minneapolis, MN: Free Spirit Publishing, Inc., 1996.

Salak, John. *Violent Crime: Is It Out of Control?* New York: Twenty-First Century Books, 1995.

Sherrow, Victoria. *Violence and the Media: The Question of Cause and Effect.* Brookfield, CT: The Millbrook Press, 1996.

Index

About the Author

Kathleen J. Edgar is a writer and editor based in the metropolitan Detroit area. She is a senior editor at a reference publisher and has edited a reference series on modern authors and another on people in the entertainment industry. She has written film reviews for various publications. She received her degree in Mass Communications from Wayne State University in Detroit.

Acknowledgements

Special thanks to Christine Tomassini for sending clippings my way.

Photo Credits

Cover photo by Olga Vega; pgs. 2, 10, 32 by Christine Innamorato; pgs. 13, 50, 56 by Ira Fox; pgs. 16, 21, 24, 26, 30 by Archive Photos; p. 19 by Archive Photos/Foto's International; p. 35 by Ron Chapple/FPG International; p.37 by Reuters/Sam Mircovich/Archive Photos; p.43 by James Levin/FPG International; p.46 by Maria Moreno.